THE HISTORY OF THE **CINCINNATI BENGALS**

Published by Creative Education

123 South Broad Street

Mankato, Minnesota 56001

Creative Education is an imprint of The Creative Company.

DESIGN AND PRODUCTION BY **EVANSDAY DESIGN**

LIBRARY OF CONGRESS CATALOGING-IN-PUBLICATION DATA

Gilbert, Sara.

The history of the Cincinnati Bengals / by Sara Gilbert.

p. cm. — (NFL today)

Summary: Traces the history of the team from its beginnings through 2003.

ISBN 1-58341-292-1

1. Cincinnati Bengals (Football team)—History—Juvenile literature.

[1. Cincinnati Bengals (Football team)—History. 2. Football—History.]

I. Title. II. Series.

GV956.C54F74 2004

796.332'64'0977178—dc22   2003065041

First edition

9 8 7 6 5 4 3 2 1

COVER PHOTO: wide receiver Chad Johnson

PHOTOGRAPHS BY

AP/Wide World Photos, Corbis (Bettmann, Wally McNamee, Reuters), Getty Images, SportsChrome USA

CINCINNATI, OHIO, WAS ESTABLISHED IN 1802 ALONG THE BANKS OF THE OHIO RIVER AND QUICKLY GREW INTO A BUSTLING PORT CITY. POET HENRY WADSWORTH LONGFELLOW CALLED IT THE "QUEEN CITY OF THE WEST," A NICKNAME THAT HAS STUCK DESPITE THE GREAT DISTANCE SEPARATING THE CITY FROM THE WEST COAST. CINCINNATI IS ALSO KNOWN FOR ITS CHILI (SERVED CINCINNATI-STYLE, ON SPAGHETTI AND TOPPED WITH CHEDDAR CHEESE) AND ITS ENDURING LOVE OF ITS PROFESSIONAL SPORTS TEAMS.

CINCINNATI'S LOVE AFFAIR WITH PRO SPORTS STARTED IN 1869, WHEN THE CITY INTRODUCED THE UNITED STATES' FIRST BASEBALL TEAM: THE CINCINNATI REDS. IN THE EARLY 1900S, CINCINNATI WAS ALSO HOME TO THREE DIFFERENT PRO FOOTBALL TEAMS, INCLUDING A CLUB KNOWN AS THE BENGALS. TWENTY-SEVEN YEARS AFTER THAT TEAM FOLDED IN 1941, LONGTIME CLEVELAND BROWNS COACH PAUL BROWN BROUGHT A NEW NATIONAL FOOTBALL LEAGUE (NFL) FRANCHISE TO CINCINNATI. IN A NOD TO THE CITY'S FOOTBALL PAST, THE NEW TEAM WAS PROMPTLY NAMED THE BENGALS.

[Wide receiver Cris Collinsworth]

PAUL BROWN WAS the Bengals' owner, general manager, and coach when the team began play in 1968. With a roster made up of veteran players taken in an expansion draft, and young players such as tight end Bob Trumpy and running back Paul Robinson, the team went 3–11 that first season.

In 1970, the team jumped to 8–6 and won the American Football Conference (AFC) Central Division title before losing in the playoffs to the Baltimore Colts. With the emergence of running back Essex Johnson, linebacker Bill Bergey, and cornerback Lemar Parrish, Coach Brown felt he had the right foundation for a championship team. The only thing missing was a talented quarterback.

Ken Anderson spent 16 seasons in Cincinnati, and his 197 touchdown passes remain a team record.

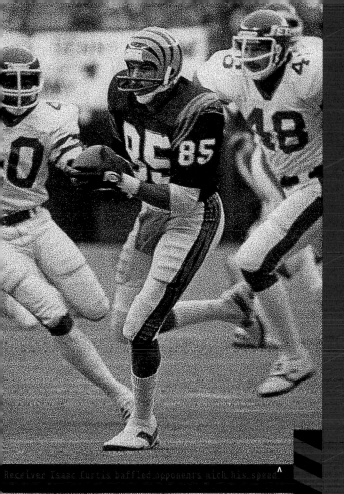

Receiver Isaac Curtis baffled opponents with his speed

Pete Johnson led the team in rushing from 1977 to 1983

In 1971, Coach Brown drafted quarterback Ken Anderson out of Augustana College to fill that role. In 1973, the young passer—with help from fullback Charles "Boobie" Clark and wide receiver Isaac Curtis—led Cincinnati to a 10–4 record and its second AFC Central title. Unfortunately, the team again lost in the first round of the playoffs.

Anderson quickly became known as one of the finest passers in football, earning his first trip to the Pro Bowl in 1975. His pinpoint accuracy was especially appreciated by Trumpy, who played with an injured elbow in 1974. "He'd throw to where I could bend my arm and catch it," Trumpy recalled. "That's how accurate he was. It was like he was saying, 'I know you can't catch with your left hand, so I'll take care of it.' And he did."

Anderson led the Bengals to their third playoff appearance in 1975 and kept the team in contention for two more seasons. But by the end of the '70s, even his best efforts and the power of bruising fullback Pete Johnson couldn't prevent Cincinnati from spiraling to the bottom of the AFC standings.

AFTER THREE STRAIGHT losing seasons, the Bengals opened the 1981 season with new, tiger-striped uniforms and helmets, and an on-field intensity to match. With hard-hitting linebacker Reggie Williams leading a stingy defense and Anderson setting new team records for most passing yards (3,754) and most touchdown passes (29) in a season, the Bengals won their division and returned to the playoffs.

Cincinnati refused to lose in the first round of the playoffs this time. The Bengals, now led by former Cleveland Browns coach Forrest Gregg, toppled the Buffalo Bills in round one. They then whipped the San Diego Chargers 27–7 in sub-zero temperatures at Cincinnati's Riverfront Stadium to win the AFC championship. Amazingly, the suddenly mighty Bengals found themselves headed to the Super Bowl.

Reggie Williams's fiery style of play helped the Bengals make the playoffs three times in the '80s.

Although Anderson set a Super Bowl record with 25 pass completions, the Bengals couldn't keep up with the high-powered San Francisco 49ers. When the clock expired, Cincinnati had lost 26–21. After the game, Coach Gregg reminded his disappointed players just how far they had come. "Everybody in Cincinnati is proud of you," he told them, "and you should take pride in yourselves."

In a 1982 season shortened by a players' strike, wide receiver Cris Collinsworth and tight end Dan Ross helped the Bengals post a 7–2 record. Unfortunately, Cincinnati then began to stumble. Although the Bengals' defense—spearheaded by Williams and speedy cornerback Ken Riley—was the toughest in the NFL, the team's offense sputtered. In 1983, the Bengals finished just 7–9.

IN 1984, THE Bengals featured two new leaders. Forrest Gregg had left town, and Sam Wyche took over as the team's new head coach. Coach Wyche's first project was a rookie quarterback named Boomer Esiason, who had been picked up in the NFL Draft.

Esiason came to the Bengals with great intelligence and confidence, and Wyche was counting on him to replace the aging Anderson. In 1985, Esiason got his chance. By the end of the season, he had thrown for 3,443 yards and 27 touchdowns. Then, with small but tough running

Boomer Esiason boosted Cincinnati with his scrambling ability, strong arm, and forceful leadership^

Early in the 1987 season, the NFL Players Association went on strike, a move that drew the anger of many football fans and slowed the momentum the Bengals had been building. Although Bengals placekicker Jim Breech had a terrific season—leading the AFC in scoring—when the players returned, Cincinnati dropped to 4–11.

Besides Breech, one of the few bright spots in Cincinnati that season was Anthony Munoz, a mountainous offensive tackle whom the Bengals had selected with the third overall pick in the 1980 NFL Draft. Munoz was blessed with an amazing combination of agility, quickness, and strength. While Cincinnati struggled in 1987, he earned a trip to the Pro Bowl for the seventh straight year.

In his 13 season with the Bengals, Munoz would be selected to 11 Pro Bowls. And in 1998, he would become the first primary Bengals player inducted into the Pro Football Hall of Fame. Kansas City Chiefs coach Marty Schottenheimer called him the best tackle of his generation. "Every guy who comes down the pike from now on will have to be compared to Anthony," said Schottenheimer. "He is the best there ever was."

MUNOZ WAS A big part of the turnaround that result-ed in a surprising 12–4 Bengals record in 1988. So was a re-energized Esiason, who had one of the best seasons of his career with 3,572 passing yards and 28 touchdown passes. Perhaps more important than either veteran, how-ever, was rookie running back Elbert "Ickey" Woods.

Woods caught the eye of the Bengals coaching staff in training camp with his nonstop hustle and earned a spot in the starting lineup. By the end of the season, he had charged for 1,066 yards and scored 15 touchdowns. He also became a fan favorite who enchanted all of Cincinnati with his strange celebratory dance. After he reached the end zone, Woods would hop on one foot, then the other, and then shake his hips for the grand finale.

Cincinnati newspapers dubbed it the "Ickey Shuffle." Everybody started doing it, from his teammates on the field to the fans in the stands. Even owner Paul Brown, who was then 80 years old, was caught shuffling once.

The 1988 Bengals had plenty of opportunities to dance as they roared to the AFC Central title. With playoff victories over the Seattle Seahawks and Buffalo Bills, Cincinnati earned its second trip to the Super Bowl, where it once again faced the San Francisco 49ers. "It's a dream come true," Woods said as the big game approached. "I'm just waiting to score and win the Super Bowl."

But there would be no dancing for Woods, and no win for the Bengals. The offense struggled to move the ball, and the defense suffered a crushing blow when star nose tackle Tim Krumrie broke his leg in the first quarter. Although the Bengals rebounded in the second half to take the lead, 49ers quarterback Joe Montana broke their hearts with a game-winning touchdown pass with 34 seconds left. "Thirty-four seconds," Coach Wyche muttered as San Francisco celebrated a 20–16 victory. "We were 34 seconds away."

Injuries plagued the Bengals the next year. Woods missed the season with a knee injury, Esiason struggled with a sore shoulder, and Krumrie wasn't as dominant as he had been before. Wide receiver Tim McGee put up 1,211 receiving yards, and James Brooks galloped for a career-best 1,239 yards, but the 1989 season ended with the Bengals out of the playoff picture.

Cincinnati rebounded in 1990, going 9–7 and crushing the Houston Oilers 41–14 in the first round of the playoffs. After that, however, everything seemed to go wrong. The 1991 season was a disastrous one that ended with a 3–13 record, and the Bengals began to rebuild. Fans didn't know it yet, but it would be a long time before they would cheer for a winner again.

IN 1992, DAVE SHULA became the NFL's youngest head coach when he was put in charge of the Bengals. His first priority was to replace the team's aging veterans with new talent. "I'm hoping to bring a new energy to this franchise," the 32-year-old coach said. "We've got a long way to go, but we're starting today."

Coach Shula soon brought in such youngsters as quarterback Jeff Blake and wide receivers Carl Pickens and Darnay Scott. Although these players had talent, their inexperience was obvious. The Bengals remained in the AFC cellar, posting 3–13 records in 1993 and 1994.

In the finest season of his NFL career, Jeff Blake passed for 3,822 yards and 28 touchdowns in 1995.

Ki-Jana Carter's promising career was cut short by injuries ^

Cincinnati hoped that running back Ki-Jana Carter—a former college star from Penn State University selected with the first overall pick in the 1995 NFL Draft—would give the team the boost it needed. But in Carter's third preseason game in 1995, he blew out a ligament in his knee and missed the entire season. The Bengals continued to sputter, and Carter would never become the star the team needed. In 1996, Shula was fired early in the season and replaced by Bruce Coslet.

With Coslet at the helm, the Bengals won seven of their last nine games in 1996 to finish a respectable 8–8. The next year, rookie running back Corey Dillon exploded onto the NFL scene with 1,129 rushing yards. Still, the Bengals finished with a losing record. Fans hoped that maybe the 1999 arrival of fleet-footed quarterback Akili Smith would change the Bengals' fortunes. But Smith struggled, Cincinnati continued to lose, and the national media began referring to the team as "the Bungles."

Corey Dillon carried Cincinnati's offense in the late 1990s ^

IN 2000, THE Bengals moved into Paul Brown Stadium, a new state-of-the-art facility on Cincinnati's riverfront. More than 64,000 fans gathered for the first regular-season game in the stadium on September 10. But as the Cleveland Browns beat the Bengals 24–7, it became obvious that it would take more than a change of scenery to make Cincinnati a winner again. Young wide receiver Peter Warrick showed signs of stardom, but the Bengals failed to climb above .500 for the 10th straight year.

The 2000 season did feature one reason for celebration in Cincinnati, however. On October 22, Dillon carved his name into the NFL record books by charging for 278 yards, the highest single-game rushing total in league history at the time. The rugged halfback finished the season with 1,435 yards, wowing teammates and opponents

Super-quick wide receiver Peter Warrick led the Bengals in catches in his first two pro seasons

Chad Johnson was one of the NFL's fastest-rising stars ^

Pro-Bowler Jon Kitna threw 26 touchdown passes in 2003 ^

alike. "He has as good a combination of size, speed, and toughness as anybody," said Tennessee Titans general manager Floyd Reese. "He's a bigger back than he gets credit for. He runs really, really hard. If you miss a tackle, he can go 80 yards."

After Cincinnati put together two more losing seasons, Marvin Lewis—who had previously been defensive coordinator for the Baltimore Ravens—was named the Bengals' new head coach. Lewis promised improvement and began building his line-up around Dillon and fellow running back Rudi Johnson, Warrick, veteran quarterback Jon Kitna, and linebacker Brian Simmons. Lewis and Bengals fans also hoped for big things from Carson Palmer, a strong-armed quarterback taken with the first overall pick in the 2003 NFL Draft.

Although more than a decade has passed since Cincinnati's last playoff appearance in 1990, the Bengals and their fans are confident that a new era is just around the corner. From Anderson to Esiason, Munoz to Dillon, Cincinnati has been home to some of the NFL's greatest players of the last three decades. Today's Bengals hope to soon run to the franchise's third Super Bowl and become the kings of football in the Queen City.

INDEX>